ABRIDGED BY LEON GARFIELD

ILLUSTRATED BY NIKOLAI SEREBRIAKOV

OTHELLO

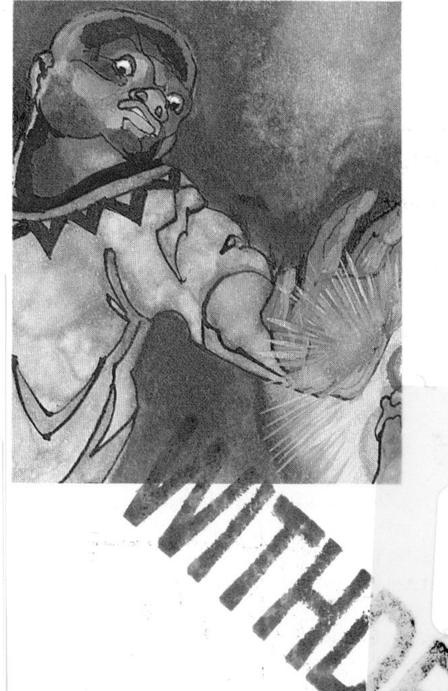

Shakespeare The Animated Tales is a multinational venture conceived by S4C, Channel 4 Wales. Produced in Russia, Wales and England, the series has been financed by S4C and the BBC (UK), Christmas Films (Russia), Home Box Office (USA) and Fujisankei (Japan).

Academic Panel
Professor Stanley Wells
Dr Rex Gibson

Educational Adviser
Michael Marland

Publishing Editor and Co-ordinator
Jane Fior

Book Design
Fiona Macmillan and Ness Wood

Animation Director for *Othello*
Nikolai Serebriakov of Christmas Films, Moscow

Series Editors
Martin Lamb and Penelope Middelboe, Right Angle, Tenby, Wales

Executive Producers
Christopher Grace (S4C)
Elizabeth Babakhina (Christmas Films)

Associate Producer
Theresa Plummer Andrews (BBC)

First published in 1994
by William Heinemann Ltd
an imprint of Reed Consumer Books Ltd
Michelin House, 81 Fulham Road, London SW3 6RB
and Auckland, Melbourne, Singapore and Toronto

Printed and bound in the UK by BPC Paulton Books Limited

First Published in 1994
Educational Supplement by Linda Marsh

BBC Educational Publishing
BBC White City, 201 Wood Lane
London W12 7TS

ISBN 0 563 39740 3

The publishers would like to thank Paul Cox for
the series logo illustration, Carol Kemp for
her calligraphy, and Rosa Fior and Celia Salisbury Jones
for their help on the books.

William Shakespeare

William Shakespeare

Next to God, a wise man once said, Shakespeare created most. In the thirty-seven plays that are his chief legacy to the world – and surely no-one ever left a richer! – human nature is displayed in all its astonishing variety.

He has enriched the stage with matchless comedies, tragedies, histories, and, towards the end of his life, with plays that defy all description, strange plays that haunt the imagination like visions.

His range is enormous: kings and queens, priests, princes and merchants, soldiers, clowns and drunkards, murderers, pimps, whores, fairies, monsters and pale, avenging ghosts 'strut and fret their hour upon the stage'. Murders and suicides abound; swords flash, blood flows, poison drips, and lovers sigh; yet there is always time for old men to talk of growing apples and for gardeners to discuss the weather.

In the four hundred years since they were written, they have become known and loved in every land; they are no longer the property of one country and one people, they are the priceless possession of the world.

His life, from what we know of it, was not astonishing. The stories that have attached themselves to him are remarkable only for their ordinariness: poaching deer, sleeping off a drinking bout under a wayside tree. There are no duels, no loud, passionate loves, no excesses of any kind. He was not one of your unruly geniuses whose habits are more interesting than their works. From all accounts, he was of a gentle, honourable disposition, a good businessman, and a careful father.

He was born on April 23rd 1564, to John and Mary Shakespeare of Henley Street, Stratford-upon-Avon. He was their third child and first son. When he was four or five he began his education at the local petty school. He left the local grammar school when he was about fourteen, in all probability to help in his father's glove-making shop. When he was eighteen, he married Anne Hathaway, who lived in a nearby village. By the time he was twenty-one, he was the father of three children, two daughters and a son.

Then, it seems, a restless mood came upon him. Maybe he travelled, maybe he was, as some say, a schoolmaster in the country; but at some time during the next seven years, he went to London and found employment in the theatre. When he was twenty-eight, he was already well enough known as an actor and playwright to excite the spiteful envy of a rival, who referred to him as 'an upstart crow'.

He mostly lived and worked in London until his mid-forties, when he returned to his family and home in Stratford, where he remained in prosperous circumstances until his death on April 23rd 1616, his fifty-second birthday.

He left behind him a widow, two daughters (his son died in childhood), and the richest imaginary world ever created by the human mind.

LEON GARFIELD

The list of the plays contained in the First Folio of 1623. This was the first collected edition of Shakespeare's plays and was gathered together by two of his fellow actors, John Hemmings and Henry Condell.

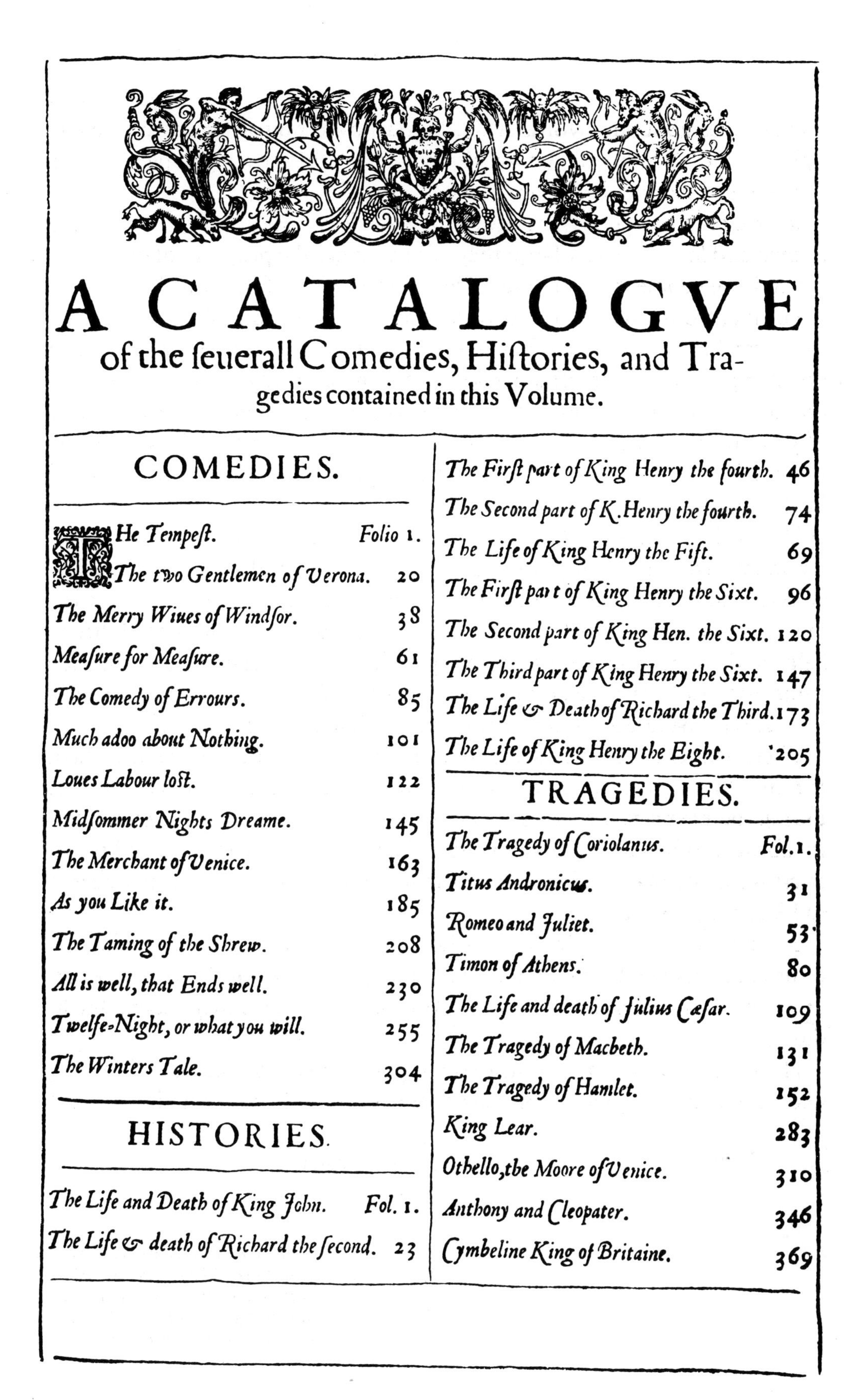

A CATALOGVE
of the ſeuerall Comedies, Hiſtories, and Tragedies contained in this Volume.

COMEDIES.

HISTORIES.

TRAGEDIES.

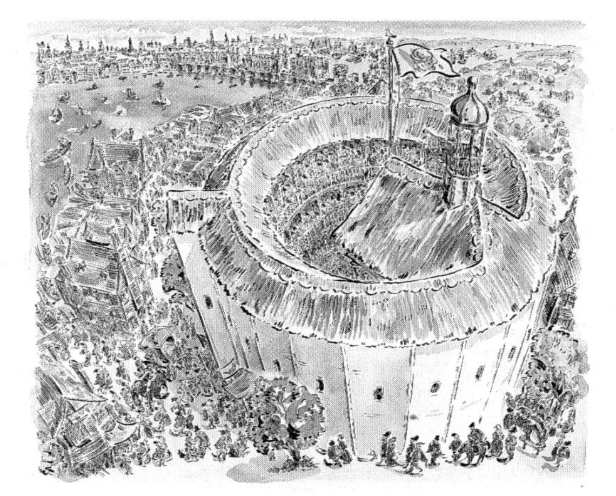

THE THEATRE IN SHAKESPEARE'S DAY

IN 1989 AN ARCHAEOLOGICAL discovery was made on the south bank of the Thames that sent shivers of delight through the theatre world. A fragment of Shakespeare's own theatre, the Globe, where many of his plays were first performed, had been found.

This discovery has fuelled further interest in how Shakespeare himself conceived and staged his plays. We know a good deal already, and archaeology as well as documentary research will no doubt reveal more, but although we can only speculate on some of the details, we have a good idea of what the Elizabethan theatre-goer saw, heard and smelt when he went to see a play by William Shakespeare at the Globe.

It was an entirely different experience from anything we know today. Modern theatres have roofs to keep out the weather. If it rained on the Globe, forty per cent of the play-goers got wet. Audiences today sit on cushioned seats, and usually (especially if the play is by Shakespeare) watch and listen in respectful silence. In the Globe, the floor of the theatre was packed with a riotous crowd of garlic-reeking apprentices, house servants and artisans, who had each paid a penny to stand for the entire duration of the play, to buy nuts and apples from the food-sellers, to refresh themselves with bottled ale, relieve themselves, perhaps, into buckets by the back wall, to talk, cheer, catcall, clap and hiss if the play did not please them.

In the galleries that rose in curved tiers around the inside of the building sat those who could afford to pay two pennies for a seat, and the benefits of a roof over their heads. Here, the middle ranking citizens, the merchants, the sea captains, the clerks from the Inns of Court, would sit crammed into their small eighteen inch space and look down upon the 'groundlings' below. In the 'Lords' room', the rich and the great, noblemen and women, courtiers and foreign ambassadors had to pay sixpence each for the relative comfort and luxury of their exclusive position directly above the stage, where they smoked tobacco, and overlooked the rest.

We are used to a stage behind an arch, with wings on either side, from which the actors come on and into which they disappear. In the Globe, the stage was a platform thrusting out into the middle of the floor, and the audience, standing in the central yard, surrounded it on three sides. There were no wings. Three doors at the back of the stage were used for all exits and entrances. These were sometimes covered by a curtain, which could be used as a prop.

Today we sit in a darkened theatre or cinema, and look at a brilliantly lit stage or screen, or we sit at home in a small, private world of our own, watching a luminous television screen. The close-packed, rowdy crowd at the Globe, where the play started at two o'clock in the afternoon, had no artificial light to enhance their illusion. It was the words that moved them. They came to listen, rather than to see.

No dimming lights announced the start of the play. A blast from a trumpet and three sharp knocks warned the audience that the action was about to begin. In the broad daylight, the actor could see the audience as clearly as the audience could see him. He spoke directly to the crowd, and held them with his eyes, following their reactions. He could play up to the raucous laughter that greeted the comical, bawdy scenes, and gauge the emotional response to the higher flights of poetry. Sometimes he even improvised speeches of his own. He was surrounded by, enfolded by, his audience.

The stage itself would seem uncompromisingly bare to our eyes. There was no scenery. No painted backdrops suggested a forest, or a castle, or the sumptuous interior of a palace. Shakespeare painted the scenery with his words, and the imagination of the audience did the rest.

Props were brought onto the stage only when they were essential for the action. A bed would be carried on when a character needed to lie on it. A throne would be let down from above when a king needed to sit on it. Torches and lanterns would suggest that it was dark, but the main burden of persuading an audience, at three o'clock in the afternoon, that it was in fact the middle of the night, fell upon the language.

In our day, costume designers create a concept as part of the production of a play into which each costume fits. Shakespeare's actors were responsible for their own costumes. They would use what was to hand in the 'tiring house' (dressing room), or supplement it out of their own pockets. Classical, medieval and Tudor clothes could easily appear side by side in the same play.

No women actors appeared on a public stage until many years after

The Workes of William Shakeſpeare,

containing all his Comedies, Hiſtories, and Tragedies: Truely ſet forth, according to their firſt ORJGJNALL.

The Names of the Principall Actors in all theſe Playes.

Illiam Shakeſpeare.

Richard Burbadge.

John Hemmings.

Auguſtine Phillips.

William Kempt.

Thomas Poope.

George Bryan.

Henry Condell.

William Slye.

Richard Cowly.

John Lowine.

Samuell Croſſe.

Alexander Cooke.

Samuel Gilburne.

Robert Armin.

William Oſtler.

Nathan Field.

John Underwood.

Nicholas Tooley.

William Eccleſtone.

Joſeph Taylor.

Robert Benfield.

Robert Goughe.

Richard Robinſon.

Iohn Shancke.

Iohn Rice.

Shakespeare's death, for at that time it would have been considered shameless. The parts of young girls were played by boys. The parts of older women were played by older men.

In 1613 the Globe theatre was set on fire by a spark from a cannon during a performance of Henry VIII, and it burnt to the ground. The actors, including Shakespeare himself, dug into their own pockets and paid for it to be rebuilt. The new theatre lasted until 1642, when it closed again. Now, in the 1990s, the Globe is set to rise again as a committed band of actors, scholars and enthusiasts are raising the money to rebuild Shakespeare's theatre in its original form a few yards from its previous site.

From the time when the first Globe theatre was built until today, Shakespeare's plays have been performed in a vast variety of languages, styles, costumes and techniques, on stage, on film, on television and in animated film. Shakespeare himself, working within the round wooden walls of his theatre, would have been astonished by it all.

PATRICK SPOTTISWOODE
Director of Education,
Globe Theatre Museum

From this list of actors, we can see that William Shakespeare not only wrote plays but also acted in them. The Globe theatre, where these actors performed, is now being rebuilt close to its original site on the south bank of the river Thames.

What They Said of Him

One will ever find, in searching his works, new cause for astonishment and admiration.

Goethe

Shakespeare was a writer of all others the most calculated to make his readers better as well as wiser.

Samuel Taylor Coleridge

An overstrained enthusiasm is more pardonable with respect to Shakespeare than the want of it; for our admiration cannot easily surpass his genius.

William Hazlitt

It required three hundred years for England to begin to hear those two words that the whole world cries in her ear – William Shakespeare.

Victor Hugo

He has left nothing to be said about nothing or anything.

John Keats

The stream of time, which is continually washing the dissoluble fabrics of other poets, passes without injury by the adamant of Shakespeare.

Samuel Johnson

Othello

This is the story of a great general, a man in whom the state of Venice has put all its trust, a black man of immense dignity and splendour who is brought to madness, murder and suicide by the skilful lies of the lieutenant he trusts and calls 'honest Iago'. "Will you, I pray," asks the tragically bewildered Othello, when Iago's villainy is discovered, "demand that demi-devil why he hath thus ensnared my soul and body?" "Demand me nothing;" answers Iago, "what you know, you know; from this time forth I never will speak word."

It is a marvellous, terrifying play, in which Shakespeare, at the very height of his powers, has created, in Iago, the most devilish villain in all drama: most devilish because, although he gives reasons for his hatred of Othello, they are too small for the monstrousness of his revenge.

The Characters in the Play

in order of appearance

Othello	*a noble Moor*
Desdemona	*daughter to Brabantio and wife to Othello*
Iago	*Othello's ensign*
Brabantio	*a senator of Venice and Desdemona's father*
Duke of Venice	
Roderigo	*a Venetian gentleman*
Cassio	*Othello's lieutenant*
Emilia	*wife to Iago and lady-in-waiting to Desdemona*
Montano	*governor of the garrison*
Bianca	*mistress to Cassio*
Lodovico	*kinsman of Brabantio*
	Sailors, officers, gentlemen and attendants

The curtain rises on a chapel. Othello the Moor, commander of all the forces of Venice, is to marry Desdemona. But it is a wedding that causes more rage than joy. Not only to Desdemona's father, Brabantio, but to Iago, Othello's ensign.

Iago	(*watching Desdemona and Othello*) I do hate him as I hate hell's pains. (*They kiss.*) O, you are well-tuned now! But I'll set down the pegs that make this music, as honest as I am.

Iago rushes through the dim and torchlit streets of Venice. He reaches Brabantio's house and bangs on the door.

Iago	Signior Brabantio, ho! Awake!
Brabantio	What is the matter there?
Iago	Look to your house, your daughter! Even now, very now, an old black ram is tupping your white ewe! Your daughter and the Moor are now making the beast with two backs!

Brabantio searches his house and discovers his daughter gone. With armed servants, he rushes through the streets to Othello's lodging and thunders on the door.

Brabantio	Who would be a father?
Othello	Keep up your bright swords for the dew will rust them!
Brabantio	O thou foul thief! Where hast thou stowed my daughter?
Othello	Where will you that I go and answer to this charge?

In the council chamber, Brabantio throws himself before the duke and accuses Othello who stands by with Iago.

BRABANTIO Oh, my daughter is abused, stolen from me and corrupted by witchcraft and medicines!

DUKE (*to Othello*)What can you say to this?

OTHELLO That I have ta'en away this old man's daughter, it is most true. True I have married her. This only is the witchcraft I have used . . . Her father loved me, oft invited me, still questioned me the story of my life. She loved me for the dangers I had passed, and I loved her, that she did pity them.

The duke and his fellow dignitaries listen entranced to Othello's adventures.

DUKE I think this tale would win my daughter too. Valiant Othello, we must straight employ you against the general enemy. You must hence tonight.

At the crowded quayside, Venetian ships make ready to set sail for Cyprus. Brabantio shouts to Othello who is already aboard.

BRABANTIO Look to her, Moor, if thou hast eyes to see: she has deceived her father and may thee! (*He points to another ship on which Desdemona stands.*)

OTHELLO My life upon her faith!

He waves to Desdemona, who waves back, with a strawberry-spotted handkerchief. Iago watches Othello and salutes him. Othello cordially returns the gesture. Roderigo, an elegant young gallant, sidles up beside Iago, gazing in a love-sick way at Desdemona.

IAGO (*nudging Roderigo suggestively*) I have told thee often, I hate the Moor. If thou canst cuckold him, thou dost thyself a pleasure, and me a sport.

Roderigo smiles hopefully, and slips some money into Iago's ready hand. He departs.

The fleet sets sail but a storm springs up and before long drives the vessels apart. The first ship to reach Cyprus carries Cassio, a young man Othello has promoted over Iago's head to be his lieutenant; then comes a vessel carrying Iago and his wife Emilia, lady-in-waiting to Othello's bride.

CASSIO (*greeting Desdemona as she disembarks*) O behold, the riches of the ship is come ashore! Hail to thee, lady!

He kneels and kisses his fingers in gallant admiration of Desdemona. She extends her hand, which Cassio takes fondly, and rises, kissing her hand as he does so.

IAGO (*aside*) Very good, well kissed, an excellent courtesy. With as little a web as this will I ensnare as great a fly as Cassio.

DESDEMONA What tidings can you tell me of my lord?

CASSIO He is not yet –

He is interrupted by a cry of 'A sail, A sail!' Desdemona looks eagerly to sea. Cassio kisses Emilia.

IAGO Sir, would she give you so much of her lips as of her tongue she oft bestows on me, you'd have enough.

DESDEMONA Alas, she has no speech!

CASSIO Lo, where he comes.

Othello appears and greets Desdemona.

OTHELLO O, my fair warrior!

DESDEMONA My dear Othello!

They embrace, as Iago looks on. Then all depart, except for Iago and Roderigo. Iago beckons to Roderigo who draws close.

IAGO Lieutenant Cassio tonight watches on the court of guard. First, I must tell thee this: Desdemona is directly in love with him.

RODERIGO I cannot believe that in her; she's full of most blest condition!

IAGO Blest pudding! Didst thou not see her paddle with the palm of his hand?

RODERIGO Well?

IAGO Do you find some occasion to anger Cassio. He's rash, and haply may strike at you. So shall you have a shorter journey to your desires . . .

It is night. In a courtyard, Cassio and a group of officers are seated round a table on which there are bottles of wine. Iago enters.

CASSIO Welcome, Iago; we must to the watch.

IAGO Not this hour, lieutenant; I have a stoup of wine –

He produces a bottle, and offers it to Cassio.

CASSIO Not tonight, good Iago; I have very poor and unhappy brains for drinking.

IAGO But one cup – (*Cassio protests and turns away. The others try to tempt him.*) If I can fasten but one cup upon him, he'll be as full of quarrel and offence as my young mistress' dog. (*Iago sees that Cassio still resists and approaches him, the bottle in hand.*) Some wine, ho! (*He seizes hold of Cassio affectionately. Music strikes up. Iago sings.*)

And let me the cannikin clink, clink.
And let me the cannikin clink;
A soldier's a man,
O, man's life's but a span,
Why then, let a soldier drink!
Why then, let a soldier drink!

Some wine . . . Cassio!

During the song, Iago begins to whirl Cassio round and round, laughingly forcing wine down his throat. The others join in. The dance becomes wild and whirling. At the height of it, Roderigo appears and taunts Cassio. Madly, drunkenly, Cassio draws his sword.

CASSIO Villain! Villain, knave!

Roderigo flees. Officers try to restrain Cassio, but he is incensed. He fights and wounds Montano. In the midst of the uproar, Othello enters.

OTHELLO Hold for your lives! What is the matter, masters? Who began this? (*They all fall back, and leave the wretched, drunken Cassio swaying, with his bloody sword in his hand. Othello looks at him sorrowfully.*) Cassio, I love thee, but never more be officer of mine.

All depart. Cassio is left alone, weeping with shame. Iago insinuates himself beside him.

IAGO What, are you hurt, lieutenant?

CASSIO Ay, past all surgery. O, I have lost the immortal part of myself. My reputation, Iago, my reputation!

IAGO As I am an honest man, I thought you had received some bodily wound.

CASSIO Drunk! And speak like a parrot! O God.

IAGO Come, come, I'll tell you what you shall do. Our general's wife is now the general. Confess yourself freely to her, importune her – she'll help to put you in your place again.

CASSIO You advise me well. I will beseech the virtuous Desdemona to undertake for me. Good night, honest Iago.

Iago smiles after him.

IAGO For whiles this honest fool plies Desdemona to repair his fortunes, and she for him pleads strongly to the Moor, I'll pour this pestilence into his ear: that she repeals him for her body's lust. So will I turn her virtue into pitch, and out of her own goodness make the net that shall enmesh them all!

Next morning, Cassio takes Iago's advice. He approaches Desdemona in the palace garden and begs her to plead his cause with Othello.

DESDEMONA Be thou assured, good Cassio, I will do all my abilities in thy behalf. (*Cassio, ever the gentleman, fervently kisses her hand. She laughs.*) Therefore be merry, Cassio –

EMILIA Madam, here comes my lord!

CASSIO (*hastily*) Madam, I'll take my leave.

He hastens away as Othello appears, accompanied by Iago. Iago glares at the retreating Cassio.

IAGO Ha! I like not that.

OTHELLO What dost thou say?

IAGO Nothing my lord.

OTHELLO Was not that Cassio that parted from my wife?

IAGO Cassio, my lord? No, sure I cannot think it, that he would steal away so guilty-like, seeing you coming.

OTHELLO I do believe 'twas he. Is he not honest?

IAGO My lord, for aught I know.

Othello stares at Iago, who shakes his head, looking at Desdemona.

OTHELLO I think so too.

IAGO Why, then I think Cassio's an honest man.

OTHELLO I know thou art full of honesty, and weigh'st thy words. Thou dost mean something . . .

IAGO Oh, beware jealousy, my lord! It is the green-eyed monster.

OTHELLO Farewell, if more thou dost perceive, let me know more. (*Iago leaves. Othello gazes towards Desdemona.*) Excellent wretch! Perdition catch my soul but I do love thee; and when I love thee not, chaos is come again!

DESDEMONA Good love, call him back.

OTHELLO Who is't you mean?

DESDEMONA Why, your lieutenant, Cassio.

OTHELLO Not now, sweet Desdemona, some other time.

DESDEMONA Shall't be tonight at supper?

OTHELLO No, not tonight.

DESDEMONA Why then, tomorrow night –

OTHELLO I do beseech thee, to leave me but a little by myself.

DESDEMONA Are you not well?

OTHELLO I have a pain upon my forehead here.

DESDEMONA Let me but bind your head, within this hour it will be well again.

OTHELLO Your napkin is too little. (*He pushes the handkerchief aside and she drops it.*) Let it alone.

Emilia, left behind, picks up the handkerchief.

EMILIA This was her first remembrance from the Moor. My wayward husband hath a hundred times wooed me to steal it; but she so loves the token –

Iago enters.

IAGO What do you here alone?

EMILIA I have a thing for you. What will you give me now for that same handkerchief?

IAGO A good wench! Give it to me. (*He snatches it.*) I will in Cassio's lodging lose this napkin and let him find it. Trifles light as air are to the jealous confirmations strong as proofs of holy writ. This may do something. The Moor already changes with my poison . . .

As he speaks, Othello approaches. His countenance is tormented as his fearful thoughts present him, over and over again, with the vision of Cassio kissing his wife's hand, until the kiss becomes lascivious.

IAGO Look where he comes! Not poppy nor mandragora, nor all the drowsy syrups of the world, shall ever medicine thee to that sweet sleep which thou owed'st yesterday.

OTHELLO (*seizing Iago by the throat*) Villain, be sure thou prove my love a whore! Or woe upon thy life!

IAGO (*freeing himself*) O grace! O heaven defend me! Take note, take note, O world! To be direct and honest is not safe.

He retreats.

OTHELLO Nay, stay; give me a living reason, that she's disloyal.

IAGO I do not like the office; but I will go on. I lay with Cassio lately. In sleep, I heard him say, 'Sweet Desdemona, let us be wary, let us hide our loves'.

OTHELLO O monstrous, monstrous!

IAGO Nay, this was but his dream –

OTHELLO I'll tear her all to pieces!

IAGO Nay, yet be wise; she may be honest yet. Have you not seen a handkerchief spotted with strawberries in your wife's hand?

OTHELLO I gave her such a one; 'twas my first gift.

IAGO I know not that; but such a handkerchief – I am sure it was your wife's – did I today see Cassio wipe his beard with.

OTHELLO O blood, Iago, blood! Within these three days let me hear thee say that Cassio's not alive.

IAGO My friend is dead: 'tis done as you request. But let her live.

OTHELLO Damn her, lewd minx! Come, go with me apart. Now art thou my lieutenant.

IAGO I am your own for ever.

In another part of the garden, Desdemona searches for the lost handkerchief. Emilia is with her.

DESDEMONA Where should I lose that handkerchief, Emilia?

EMILIA I know not, madam.

Othello enters.

DESDEMONA	How is't with you, my lord?
OTHELLO	I have a salt and sorry rheum offends me; lend me thy handkerchief.
DESDEMONA	Here, my lord.
OTHELLO	That which I gave you.
DESDEMONA	I have it not about me.
OTHELLO	That's a fault. That handkerchief did an Egyptian to my mother give. She told her, while she kept it, 'twould subdue my father entirely to her love; but if she lost it or made a gift of it, my father's eye should hold her loathly . . .
DESDEMONA	Then would to God that I had never seen't!
OTHELLO	Is't lost? Is't gone?

DESDEMONA Heaven bless us! This is a trick to put me from my suit. Pray you let Cassio be received again.

OTHELLO Fetch me that handkerchief.

DESDEMONA I pray, talk me of Cassio.

OTHELLO The handkerchief!

He rushes away like a madman. But the handkerchief has gone. Iago has put it in Cassio's lodging and Cassio, finding it and liking it, has given it to Bianca, his mistress, to copy.

Still searching for the handkerchief, Desdemona and Emilia leave the garden and presently Iago and Othello enter together. Othello leans almost pathetically, towards his new lieutenant. He is sweating and seems unwell.

OTHELLO What hath he said?

IAGO Faith, that he did – I know not what he did.

OTHELLO But, what?

IAGO Lie –

OTHELLO With her?

IAGO With her, on her, what you will.

OTHELLO Lie with her? Lie on her? Handkerchief – confessions – handkerchief! Is't possible? O devil!

During the above wild outburst. Othello is overwhelmed by hateful fancies, which finally dissolve into a red oblivion, like the fires of hell. Gradually the fragmented images solidify into Iago's face, looking down, much concerned.

IAGO How is it, general? Whilst you were here, mad with your grief, Cassio came hither. I shifted him away; bade him anon return and here speak with me. Do but encave yourself, for I will make him tell the tale anew, where, how, how oft, how long ago, and when he has and is again to cope your wife. Will you withdraw?

Othello, helplessly in the power of Iago, nods and hides himself behind a trellis, like a netted beast. Cassio approaches.

IAGO (*to himself*) Now will I question Cassio of Bianca. As he shall smile, Othello shall go mad.

Iago, with the skill of a dancer, leads Cassio, whispering in his ear, close to the trellis behind which Othello listens.

IAGO (*to Cassio, aloud*) I never knew a woman love man so.

CASSIO (*laughing*) Alas, poor rogue! I think i' faith she loves me. She hangs and lolls and weeps upon me, so hales and pulls me . . .

OTHELLO Now he tells how she plucked him to my chamber. O, I see that nose of yours, but not the dog I shall throw it to!

Bianca enters. She is clutching the handkerchief.

BIANCA (*flourishing it*) This is some minx's token, and I must take out the work? There!

OTHELLO By heaven, that should be my handkerchief!

Bianca throws the handkerchief at Cassio, and stalks away indignantly.

IAGO After her, after her!

CASSIO Faith, I must. She'll rail in the streets else. (*He follows.*)

OTHELLO (*emerging from concealment*) How shall I murder him, Iago? I would have him nine years a-killing. A fine woman, a fair woman, a sweet woman!

IAGO Nay, you must forget that.

OTHELLO No, my heart is turned to stone. I strike it, and it hurts my hand. O, the world hath not a sweeter creature! O Iago, the pity of it, Iago!

IAGO If you are so fond over her iniquity –

OTHELLO Get me some poison, Iago, this night. This night, Iago!

IAGO Do it not with poison; strangle her in her bed, even the bed she hath contaminated. And for Cassio, let me be his undertaker.

OTHELLO Good, good! The justice of it pleases.

A trumpet sounds. The two men stare. At the harbour, Lodovico, the ambassador from the duke, disembarks and is greeted by Desdemona. Othello, accompanied by Iago, appears and Lodovico gives him a letter.

LODOVICO (*to Othello*) The Duke and Senators of Venice greet you. (*To Desdemona*) How does Lieutenant Cassio?

Frowning, Othello moves away, reading.

DESDEMONA Cousin, there's fallen between him and my lord an unkind breach; I would do much to atone them, for the love I bear to Cassio.

OTHELLO Devil! (*He strikes her.*)

DESDEMONA (*weeping*) I have not deserved this.

LODOVICO (*comforting her*) Maybe the letter moved him for as I think they do command him home. (*To Othello*) My lord, make her amends; she weeps.

OTHELLO O devil, devil! Out of my sight! (*Bewildered, Desdemona departs.*) Sir, I obey the mandate, and will return to Venice.

Othello rushes away.

LODOVICO (*to Iago*) Is this the noble Moor whom our full senate call all-in-all sufficient? Are his wits safe?

IAGO Alas, alas! It is not honesty in me to speak what I have seen and known. Do but go after and mark how he continues . . .

Desdemona's bedchamber. She is seated with Emilia. Othello enters.

OTHELLO Let me see your eyes; look in my face. (*He dismisses Emilia with a wave of his hand. She goes.*) What art thou?

DESDEMONA Your wife, my lord, your true and loyal wife.

OTHELLO Are you not a strumpet?

DESDEMONA No, as I shall be saved!

OTHELLO I cry you mercy. I took you for that cunning whore of Venice that married with Othello.

He rushes from the room. Emilia returns with Iago, to comfort Desdemona.

EMILA How do you, madam?

IAGO What is the matter, my lady?

EMILIA He called her whore.

DESDEMONA O good Iago, what shall I do to win my lord again?

IAGO 'Tis but his humour, the business of the state does him offence, and he does chide with you. Weep not, all things shall be well. (*He leaves.*)

DESDEMONA (*as Emilia unpins her hair and begins to brush it.*) How foolish are our minds! My mother had a maid called Barbary, and he she loved proved mad, and did forsake her; she had a song of 'willow', and she died singing it; that song tonight will not go from my mind.

EMILIA Come, come, you talk.

DESDEMONA (*singing*)

The poor soul sat sighing by a sycamore tree,
Sing all a green willow;
Her hand on her bosom, her head on her knee,
Sing willow, willow, willow,
Sing willow, willow, willow,
Must be my garland . . .

As she sings, Othello, by an open window, hears the song faintly. He frowns and stares down into the dark town below. There, Iago waits in the street near the palace for Roderigo.

IAGO If thou hast purpose, courage, valour, then this night show it.

RODERIGO I have no great devotion to the deed . . .

IAGO Fear nothing, I'll be at thy elbow.

Cassio bids farewell to Bianca and comes out into the street.

IAGO (*to himself*) Whether he kill Cassio, or Cassio him, or each do kill the other, every way makes my game.

A scuffle of shadows. Roderigo attacks Cassio. He falls and is himself wounded. He crawls away. Iago darts forward and stabs Cassio from behind, and then vanishes into concealment. There are shouts and cries.

CASSIO Help, ho! Murder, murder!

Othello, still by the window, hears the shout.

OTHELLO The voice of Cassio: Iago keeps his word. O brave Iago, thou hast such noble sense of thy friend's wrong! Thou teachest me . . . (*He leaves the room.*)

The street is alive with torches and anxious faces, surrounding the wounded Cassio. Among them are Lodovico and Iago.

IAGO O my lieutenant! What villains have done this?

A voice calls from the shadows.

RODERIGO'S VOICE O, help me here!

CASSIO That's one of them!

IAGO (*finding Roderigo*) O murderous slave! (*He stabs him.*)

RODERIGO O damned Iago! O inhuman dog! (*He dies.*)

IAGO (*staring up towards the castle from which Othello has looked down*) This is the night that either makes me, or fordoes me quite.

In her bedchamber, Desdemona lies on her bed. She closes her eyes. Quietly, Othello enters. He gazes first at the sleeping Desdemona, then at the candle beside her.

OTHELLO Put out the light, and then put out the light: if I quench thee, thou flaming minister, I can again thy former light restore, should I repent me; but once put out thy light – (*He frowns, then bends to kiss her.*)

DESDEMONA Othello?

OTHELLO Ay, Desdemona.

DESDEMONA Will you come to bed, my lord?

OTHELLO Have you prayed tonight, Desdemona?

DESDEMONA Ay, my lord.

OTHELLO If you bethink yourself of any crime unreconciled as yet to heaven and grace, solicit for it straight. I would not kill thy unprepared spirit.

DESDEMONA Then heaven have mercy on me!

OTHELLO The handkerchief which I so loved, and gave thee, thou gavest to Cassio.

DESDEMONA I never gave it him, send for him hither –

OTHELLO He has confessed.

DESDEMONA What, my lord?

OTHELLO That he hath . . . used thee.

DESDEMONA He will not say so!

OTHELLO No, his mouth is stopped.

DESDEMONA Alas, he is betrayed, and I undone!

Othello seizes a pillow.

OTHELLO Down, strumpet!

DESDEMONA Kill me tomorrow, let me live tonight!

OTHELLO Nay, an' you strive –

DESDEMONA But half an hour!

OTHELLO It is too late!

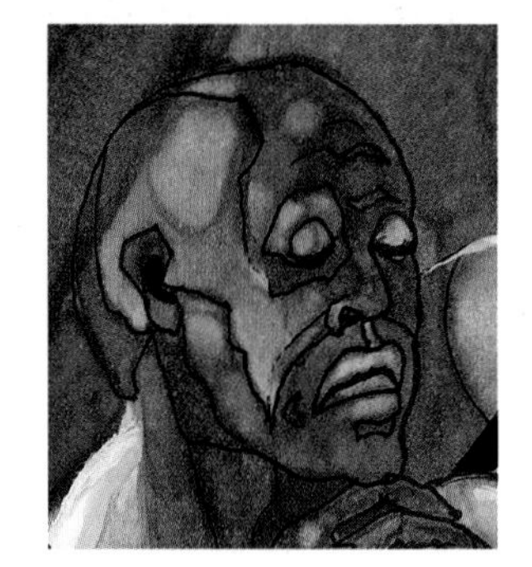

He presses the pillow down on her face to suffocate her. There is a knocking on the door.

EMILIA'S VOICE My lord, my lord!

OTHELLO 'Tis Emilia! If she come in, she'll sure speak to my wife – my wife, my wife! What wife? I have no wife! O insupportable –

EMILIA I do beseech you that I may speak with you!

OTHELLO O, come in, Emilia.

He draws the bed curtains and goes to unlock the door. Emilia enters and moves towards the bed.

DESDEMONA (*faintly*) O falsely, falsely murdered!

EMILIA (*rushing to draw back the bed curtains*) O, lady, speak again! Who hath done this deed?

DESDEMONA Nobody; I myself. Commend me to my kind lord. O farewell. (*She dies.*)

OTHELLO She's like a liar gone to burning hell: 'twas I that killed her!

EMILIA O, the more angel she, and you the blacker devil!

OTHELLO She was as false as water!

EMILIA Thou as rash as fire to say that she was false!

OTHELLO Cassio did top her: ask thy husband else.

EMILIA My husband?

OTHELLO Ay, 'twas he that told me first –

EMILIA My husband?

OTHELLO I say thy husband. My friend, thy husband, honest, honest Iago.

EMILIA If he say so, may his pernicious soul rot half a grain a day! Help, help, ho! help! The Moor hath killed my mistress!

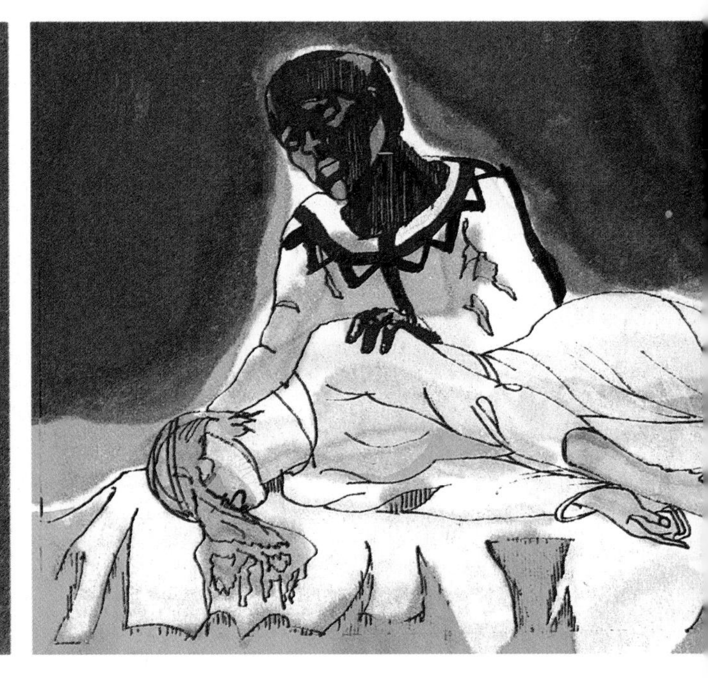

Montano and Iago burst into the room. They see the murdered Desdemona.

MONTANO O monstrous act!

OTHELLO 'Tis pitiful; but yet Iago knows that she with Cassio hath the act of shame a thousand times committed. Cassio confessed it, and she did gratify his amorous works with the recognisance and pledge of love which I first gave her. I saw it in his hand: it was a handkerchief.

EMILIA 'Twill out, it will out! O thou dull Moor, that handkerchief thou speakest on I found by fortune and did give my husband. He begged of me to steal it –

IAGO Filth, thou liest!

He stabs Emilia from behind, and escapes. Emilia falls, dying, on the bed. Montano pursues Iago.

EMILIA (*dying*) Moor, she was chaste; she loved thee, cruel Moor.

She dies. Othello gazes down upon the dead Desdemona. With horror he begins to understand the full extent of Iago's treachery.

OTHELLO O ill-starred wench! Pale as thy smock! When we shall meet at compt this look of thine will hurl my soul from heaven and fiends will snatch at it. Cold, cold my girl, even like thy chastity.

Montano, Lodovico, and the wounded Cassio enter with Iago, guarded. Othello stares at Iago, and approaches him.

OTHELLO If that thou be'st a devil, I cannot kill thee. (*He wounds him with his sword. At once, soldiers disarm him.*)

IAGO I bleed, sir, but not killed.

LODOVICO This wretch hath part confessed his villainy.

CASSIO Dear general, I did never give you cause.

OTHELLO I do believe it, and I ask your pardon. Will you, I pray, demand that demi-devil why he hath thus ensnared my soul and body?

IAGO Demand me nothing; what you know, you know. From this time forth I never will speak word.

LODOVICO (*to Othello*) You must forsake this room and go with us –

OTHELLO Soft you, a word or two. I have done the state some service and they know't. I pray you in your letters when you shall these unlucky deeds relate, speak of them as they are; nothing extenuate nor set down aught in malice. Then must you speak of one that loved not wisely, but too well. Set you down this; and say besides that in Aleppo once where a malignant and a turbaned Turk beat a Venetian and traduced the state, I took by the throat the circumcised dog and smote him thus! (*He stabs himself and falls beside Desdemona.*) I kissed thee ere I killed thee: no way but this, killing myself, to die upon a kiss.

The curtain falls.

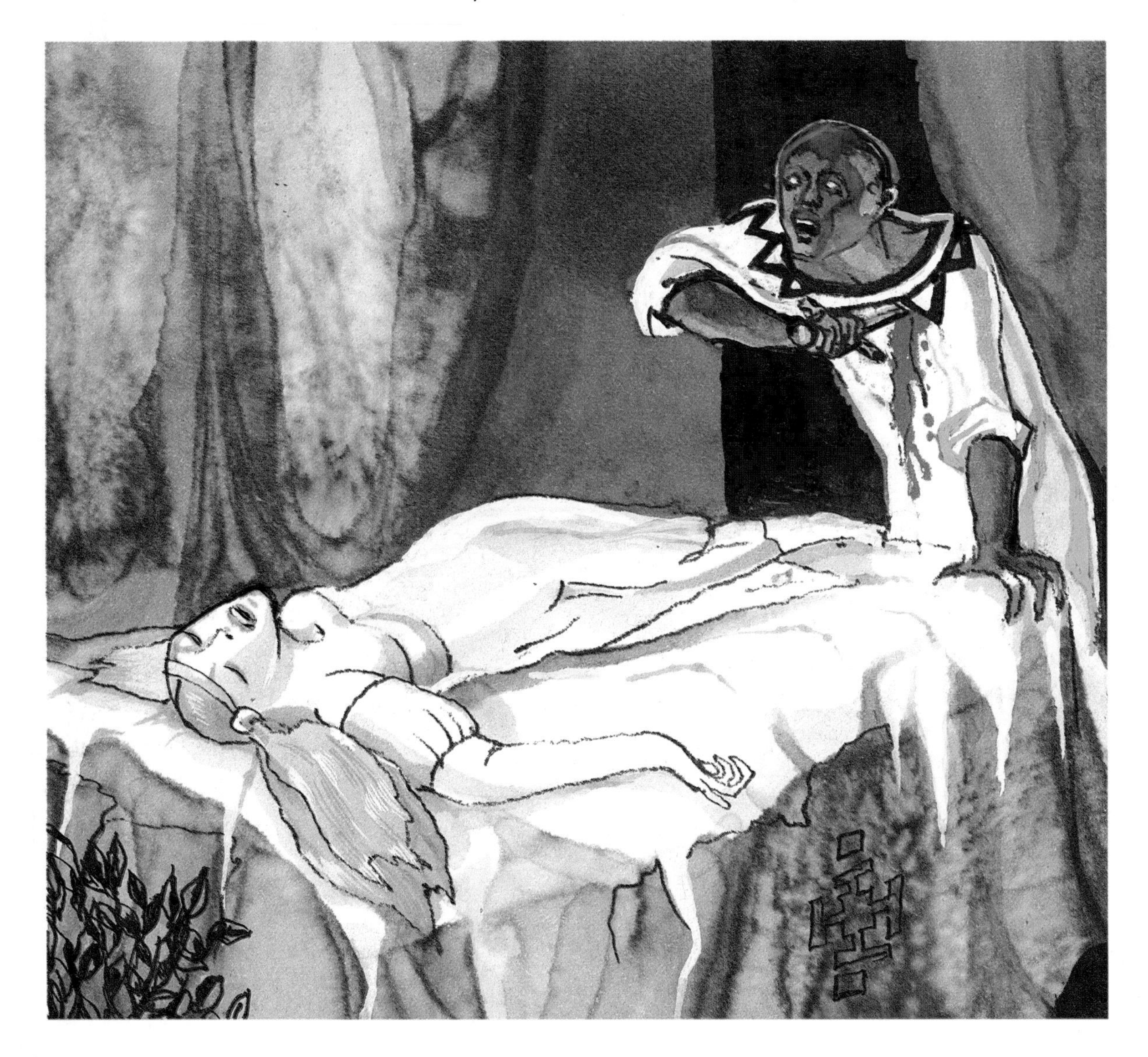

OTHELLO

THE PLAY, THE ANIMATED VIDEO, THE AUTHOR, AND HIS TIMES

Study assignments by Linda Marsh, English Department, North Westminster Community School, London

When you watch *Othello* for the first time, it has something of the quality of a thriller. Why does Iago say 'I hate the Moor'? How far will his hatred take him? Othello himself flashes from love to suspicion, then from anger to murder. Even in the bedchamber scene, events tug us along in a current of fear and despair, and yet it seems as if someone must come in and stop it all. Margaret Webster, who directed the play in New York in 1943, remembers a girl in the audience whispering over and over again, 'Oh God, don't let him kill her... don't let him kill her...' You read, or you watch, straining for an ending in which justice is done and innocent people are rescued in time so they can live happily afterwards.

When you are more familiar with the story, its ending is almost obvious from the beginning. We are drawn more deeply into Othello's passion and Desdemona's sorrow; the terrible pity of it all. The play powerfully teaches us about doubt and jealousy, and how it is possible to lose sight of a loved one in the shadows of our own concerns and furies.

So although written for a particular kind of theatre (the open-stage as shown on page 54) and for the London audiences of the late sixteenth and early seventeenth century, Shakespeare's *Othello* is for all times, and can be enjoyed in many different media: sound recordings, films, books or different kinds of productions in different kinds of theatres. The television series on which this book is based is a new approach: animations devised by Russian artists, spoken by a British cast of actors, and using Shakespeare's actual words in a specially prepared version.

The following assignments have been planned for you to use with your teacher to help you think more about the play. They include work on:

• its story, its characters, and the language they speak;
• the ideas and themes from *Othello* and their connection with many aspects of life today;
• the artistic approach to the play in sixteenth and seventeenth-century England, in other productions at other times, and in this animated version.

Some of the assignments ask you to re-read the text or to research. Others invite you to act, and others to write. All of them ask you to think about the play - its words and ideas. Some you will be able to carry out only with the help of your teacher, but others you can do at school or at home after watching the programmes or video and reading the script. The assignments are grouped into sections according to the aspect of the play being considered, but obviously your teacher will not wish you simply to work through them in order, and each of you can create your own study pattern from the range of assignments.

I hope that these assignments will help you to understand and enjoy the animated version of *Othello* better, to re-read the text with greater enjoyment, and to learn more about Shakespeare and his theatre.

L.M.

*T*HE *S*TUDY *A*SSIGNMENTS

IAGO

1 *The great operatic composer, Verdi, wrote an opera based on Shakespeare's play* Othello, *and in the early stages of his thinking he decided to call it 'Iago'. Later, he changed his mind, and it became 'Otello' (the Italian version of the name). But he was gripped by the terrible tension between the two men, and at times felt the play's dramatic force lived more powerfully in Iago.*

In one of the scenes in his opera, Othello falls to his knees swearing vengeance. Iago prevents him from rising, also kneeling to swear. Only when they sing together does the audience realize that it is Iago who has the melody (the strong, tuneful part of the music). He literally 'calls the tune', while Othello accompanies the line contrapuntally (a second tune working in with the first).

1.a With a partner, look at the lines on page 24 from 'Ha! I like not that' to '...chaos is come again'. Each taking a part, play the scene to:

• give Othello the greater strength and presence of the two. Iago should 'try his luck', attempt to goad him, but find Othello difficult to move.
• give the scene to Iago. Just a little push and Othello topples into the trap.

1.b Some of you can read aloud your interpretations to the rest of the class. Listen carefully each time to see if you can identify any lines which particularly allow readers or actors to claim that the scene 'belongs' to either Othello or Iago. For example, Othello's words 'I think so too' could be read with doubt or conviction, couldn't they?

2 *In 1694, Charles Gildon wrote (in his 'Miscellaneous Letters and Essays') that he had it '...from very good hands that the person that acted Iago was in much esteem for a comedian to make the audience laugh, who had not learnt to be serious a whole play.'*

Later, Samuel Sandford played the part of Iago as nastily as possible, although at some cost to his reputation, because audiences were shy of applauding great villainous acting in case they should be seen as taking sides with that character.

2.a Look through the script and choose some lines which allow you to:

• play Iago with a light touch, deftly drawing the attention to his manipulative skills in a way which might fascinate and amuse us.
• give full scope to Iago's evil presence, allowing us to see and hear, almost touch and taste, the part he plays in the tragedy.

2.b Try out your interpretations on a partner. See if she or he agrees with you.

STAGING OTHELLO

3 *Some directors are inclined to make Iago too wicked.*

Verdi, for instance, wrote that if he were an actor and had to play Iago, he would rather have '...an absent, nonchalant manner, indifferent to everything, witty, speaking good and evil almost lightheartedly...' so that if anyone were to suggest he were capable of wickedness, he could say, 'Really?' and shake off the notion with laughter. Only this kind of figure could deceive everyone in the way Iago really does. Verdi felt that to play Iago more openly as a force for evil would make Othello look a fool. After all, if someone is obviously bad, it makes sense to mistrust and avoid him.

3.a What evidence is there in the script that Iago:

• delights in controlling others?
• is indifferent to their pain?

Working with a partner, write down any lines which you feel fit under these two headings.

3.b Return to the scene described in the second point under **1.a** and imagine that you are Iago thinking about it afterwards. Are you merely mischievous or is there a deeper evil at work in you? Write down your thoughts.

3.c Many people think that Iago sets out as the master of his own plot, creating it out of whatever comes to hand. Then he gets in too far, and it masters him. Where in the play might this be happening? Macbeth, in another of Shakespeare's great tragedies, says, after yet another murder in pursuit of his ambition to be king, 'I am in blood stepped in so far, that should I wade no more, returning were as tedious as go o'er.' He's come so far that he may as well keep going. Find a point in the script when Iago might turn, as if to the audience, and admit that he is trapped into seeing the story through. What might he then say? Write down these lines.

3.d Shakespeare gives to Macbeth, as he does to Othello, a sense of loss that dawns on him when he reaches the point of no return. Macbeth has these hauntingly beautiful lines to say:

'Had I but died an hour before this chance
I had lived a blessed time, for from this instant
There's nothing serious in mortality.
All is but toys. Renown and grace is dead.
The wine of life is drawn, and the mere lees
Is left this vault to brag of.'

For Othello, this moment comes after Desdemona's death, with Emilia's voice ringing in his ears, when he can suddenly 'see' his soul hurled from heaven. Cassio calls him 'Dear general', putting before his title that adjective which he has never used before and through which the fullness of his sorrow and pity for Othello is acutely registered. No one looks at Iago with such love, and he, of all the people in the room, stands friendless, the object of horror. What do you think is going through his mind at that point? And what do you think is going to happen to him?

4 *In 1833, the great actors Kean and Macready were billed to swap parts as Othello and Iago. Kean did not act the part of Iago because he didn't want to lose the sympathies of the audience. Macready also directed the performance as well as playing one or the other parts. He so placed the actors that whichever part he was acting, whether Othello or Iago, he was in front blotting out the other.*

The theatres in which they acted were quite different from the early Elizabethan theatres. You can see from the drawing overleaf that the stage jutted out into the audience.

The Swan Theatre, 1596

The great Victorian theatres of our towns and cities that still exist and are popular today, and many modern theatres built like them, are quite different: the performers work behind a proscenium arch, with the audience looking through a specially lit opening into another world - the stage, its actors and scenery. The nineteenth century, therefore, distanced the performers by creating a sharp line between actors and audience. This is quite unlike the mixing of the Elizabethan London theatre or the African or Asian theatre. The proscenium stage looks like this:

Mander and Mitcheson Theatre Collection

This means that the audience watches at some distance from the stage and feels more separate from the performance. But the shape into which the Elizabethan audience was pressed around the stage created a close and vivid relationship between the actors and the audience. Some producers today choose a smaller theatre to help the laughter along or to encourage the warmth of feeling of the drama, to draw people into the play's sadness or its dramatic effects. The television 'close-up' and the character's speaking directly to the audience through the screen is in many ways a modern equivalent of the Elizabethan soliloquy. In a strange way the technology of the Elizabethan theatre was rather like that of modern television: it brought the actor very close to the audience.

4.a As a director, where on the Elizabethan stage would you put Iago and Cassio as they talk and laugh together, beginning with Iago's words on page 33: 'I never knew a woman love man so.' Where would you put Othello while he hides and listens? Who will you put closest to the audience? Draw a diagram and explain your reasons.

4.b Where would you stage the bedchamber scene in which Desdemona dies?

OTHELLO

5 *Verdi chooses to put into Act I of his opera, 'Otello', a love duet sung by Othello and Desdemona which immediately establishes the depth and beauty of their relationship over and above everything else. In the animated version of Shakespeare's* Othello, *we meet them after they have met and declared their love for each other, and we are taken very quickly to the point where Othello has begun to doubt her. In this version, how readily did you believe that they truly loved one another?*

5.a Brabantio and Iago do their best to convince us that this love is not right and will not last. Look through the script from the beginning to Othello's lines: 'My life upon her faith!' Write down the points they make and the feelings they express about the lovers.

5.b We know that Iago is out to make mischief, but Brabantio is truly amazed and outraged. He probably finds the Duke's response to Othello's tales of his adventures a further cause for anger and dismay. If Brabantio were given the chance to talk to the Duke alone, what might he say to him? Write this scene.

5.c What is it about these lines of Othello's in the script and in the portrayal of Othello in the animated version that balances the disbelief of others and gives him our confidence? Write about four or five lines summarizing the peculiar power of his speech and presence as if you were an onlooker, giving a statement of what you saw and experienced.

from A.C. Bradley *Shakespeare's Tragedies* ed Lerner (Pelican 1963).

6 *The famous critic A. C. Bradley, writing earlier this century, described Othello as coming before us:*

> *'...dark and grand, no longer young and now grave, self-controlled, steeled by experience of countless perils, hardships, simple and stately in bearing and speech. He is unawed by dignitaries, unelated by honours, and he comes to have his life*

crowned with the final glory of love, a love as strange, adventurous and romantic as any passage of his eventful history. Once convinced, he will act with the authority of a judge and the swiftness of a man in mortal pain. Undeceived he will do like execution on himself. He is trustful and thorough in his trust.'

This is a view of Othello that has frequently been upheld by actors. When Edmund Kean spoke the farewell scene, it was described as being like 'the last breeze of summer sighing among the branches of the cypress grove...like the hollow and not unmusical murmur of the midnight sea' (Blackwoods Magazine, *March 1818).*

6.a This is a noble view of Othello that draws us into his anguish. But what if you felt angry with him, and wanted to demonstrate his weaknesses, his errors of judgement, his harshness towards the very person he should have loved most in all the world? What description would you write then? See what you can produce.

7 *One of the first points that Iago makes about Othello has reference to his blackness. 'An old black ram is tupping your white ewe' is meant to shock. Long ago, even the great poet Coleridge thought 'it would be something monstrous to conceive this beautiful Venetian girl falling in love with a veritable negro.'*

Othello may be older than Desdemona, and come from another country: two facts for Brabantio to worry about and for others to ponder. But if he were, say, Portuguese, would the father have been so wholly thrown? There is no sense that anyone, even Brabantio, thinks Desdemona is lowering herself socially in marrying Othello, because he is revered as a formidable general. It is his blackness that startles them, and his blackness that suddenly becomes a presumption as he looks to be Desdemona's suitor and by implication seeks to enter her family and community, rather than just to protect them.

In the years since it was written, this issue has been at the heart of the play and proved a special challenge for actors and directors.

7.a How black should Othello be? This is a far from stupid question for those putting on the play in places where racism is rampantly alive. Take areas such as the deep south of America, for example, where black people have a history of slavery and where the Ku Klux Klan still roam. A white audience there might wish to see a black man brought down. Should you, therefore, play down his blackness, in case his tragedy be thought to stem from his ethnicity? Should you play it up? A black actor with Othello's power and presence might move across barriers and strike the hearts of at least some of the people watching, despite the risks involved in a politicized production.

In small groups, pick a place and imagine you are a director, with a group of sponsors, wishing to put on a production of *Othello*. Discuss the options open to you and each of their risks and consequences. Elect a spokesperson to describe your situation to the rest of the class and summarize your conclusions.

8 *On the Sunday before the opening night of* Othello *at the Savoy Theatre in 1930, when Paul Robeson, the celebrated black American actor, and Peggy Ashcroft played the lead parts, an interview appeared in 'The Observer' in which Robeson stated his belief that the play turned on racial prejudice: 'It is a tragedy of racial conflict; a tragedy of honour rather than of jealousy... it is because he is an alien among white people that his mind works so quickly, for he feels dishonour more deeply...' And he added that he found in Shakespeare 'a superb sympathy for the underdog'.*

One critic said of his performance that the fact that he was black 'seemed to floodlight the whole drama...new points, new nuances were constantly emerging.' This was in contrast to a whole history of white actors with painted faces.

Thirteen years later, Robeson took a touring production of Othello *to America, where he refused to play to segregated audiences. Race riots were happening, and each night when he first kissed Desdemona, the audience gasped. But 'everywhere we went, Robeson was adored', wrote his stage manager, Francis Letton. 'Every night long lines of people waited to speak to him - black and white... and he spoke with every one of them. He was a truly great man.'*

8.a Discuss the following in small groups:

• Could the effect that Robeson had on his audience in those places and at that time have been achieved by a powerful white actor reasonably painted?
• Can it ever be appropriate in the twentieth century for a white actor to play Othello? One black member of an audience rose to applaud the distinguished white actor, Laurence Olivier, because 'obviously it was done with love'. What do you think? (Can black actors ever play parts for white men and women?)
• Would it make any difference to the play if it were performed with an entirely black cast?
• In 1852, the black American actor, Ira Aldridge, played Othello in Russian. He moved a critic to say that in Aldridge's misery 'is heard the far-off groans of his own people oppressed by unbelievable slavery, and more than that - the groans of the whole of suffering mankind.' This suggests that a black actor may embody a sense of the weight of black history and yet also Othello's sheer humanity; that Othello is a man as well as black, and that he speaks for the pain of all human beings. Do you agree, or not?
• Why do you think Shakespeare made Othello black?

Willard White as Othello (BBC 1990)

8.b Now, by yourself, design a poster for a production of *Othello*. It should bring out the aspect of Othello's identity which suggests itself most strongly to you. Work with your own drawings, a montage of pictures from newspapers and magazines, or any other medium that suits you.

DESDEMONA

9 *Desdemona is often pictured as Othello's passive victim, but here are some points to consider that give an alternative view:*

- *She persists in pleading for Cassio even when she sees the warning light in Othello's eyes.*
- *Othello himself calls her 'my fair warrior'!*
- *She has had the courage to defy her father and marry a man to whom her 'natural' reaction was expected to be fear, not delight. This would have been a massive act of will, a very brave and unusual choice.*
- *She took responsibility for her death to save Othello at the last; her love was absolute.*

9.a The stage directions tell us on page 40 that Desdemona 'lies on her bed. She closes her eyes.' In all this turmoil, what thoughts are uppermost in her mind? Write them down.

9.b Do you think she had any choice in submitting to Othello when he came into her room? She puts up a kind of struggle, pleading for her life just for that night, and then for half an hour. See if you can think of another single phrase, in keeping with the quiet strength of her character, that might have stopped him in his tracks, if only for a moment.

9.c Othello says to Emilia, 'I have no wife! O insupportable'. What exactly is insupportable? Something more than blind jealousy has begun to work its way through to the surface of his mind, even though at this point he still believes her to be guilty. What might it be?

THE HANDKERCHIEF

10 *Much of the plot turns on the business of the handkerchief. Once in rehearsal, Margaret Webster, playing Emilia, came on to the stage to find that there was no handkerchief to pick up. In a flash, the rest of the play went through her mind - 'No handkerchief, no play. I couldn't give it to Iago, he couldn't plant it on Cassio, Othello couldn't see Cassio give it to Bianca, Iago couldn't use it to prove Desdemona's guilt... the whole play fell to pieces like a pack of cards.'*

It is Othello's only 'evidence'. Everything else is hearsay and speculation.

10.a How willing or reluctant do you think Othello is to believe that Desdemona has given it away? Read these lines aloud to a partner, firstly with sincerity and trust, then with disbelief, then anger:

'I gave her such a one; 'twas my first gift' (page 28).

'Fetch me that handkerchief' (page 30).

Which sounds most convincing to you?

10.b Set the play in modern times. Write the scene in which he confronts Desdemona with his suspicions or what he thinks of as his evidence. (You may wish to substitute something else for the handkerchief.) Will your Desdemona react differently? Will Othello have the same authority?

SHAKESPEARE'S SOURCE

11 *Shakespeare's source for* Othello *was 'Hecatommithi' by Cinthio, published in Venice in 1566. In Cinthio's version, Iago has no hatred for Othello; his motives are lust and then hatred for Desdemona. It is her ruin, not Othello's, that he wants.*

Another important change occurs in the scene where Desdemona is killed. Cinthio makes Othello and Iago murder her together, and then they try to cover it up by making out that the ceiling has fallen and crushed her.

11.a What differences do Shakespeare's changes make to our understanding of the story, and do you think they work for the better?

11.b If you were retelling the story, what changes would *you* make? Write them down and compare your ideas with the rest of the class. Does anyone come up with an idea that really strikes the rest of you?

WOMEN

12 *In 1660, one of the changes introduced into the world of theatre was that of women actresses. Many of the actors used to the tradition of 'men only' performances were astonished and some even petitioned the king to go back to the old ways of men playing female parts. It was as Desdemona that the first professional woman actress appeared on stage. Towards the end of 1660, this prologue was written:*

'I come, unknown to any of the rest
To tell you news - I saw the lady dressed.
The woman plays today, mistake me not,
No man in gown or page in petticoat;
A woman to my knowledge, yet I can't,
If I should die, make affidavit on't.
In this reforming age
We have intents to civilise the stage.
Our women are defective, and so sized
You'd think they were some of the Guard disguised.
For (to speak truth) men act, that are between
Forty and fifty, wenches of fifteen;
With bone so large and nerve so incompliant,
When you call Desdemona, enter Giant.'

This prologue makes fun of the custom, but we know that there were some men who could play women very persuasively. It was even said of the actor Kynaston 'that it has since been disputable among the judicious whether any woman that succeeded him so sensibly touched the audience as he.' ('Sensibly' here meaning 'with feelings'.)

12.a As a modern director of a television production, who would you like to cast as Desdemona and Emilia, and why?

12.b If one of your aims in your production was to convince audiences that the play contained powerful scenes with and for women, which scene would you choose as a trailer? Which line or lines from this scene might you emphasize?

LOVE

13 *If Othello had a fantasy of a woman in his mind when he married Desdemona, then the reality of her real, warm, growing, changing self would always have shaken him. To think that she was unfaithful made him utterly frantic.*

Here is one of Shakespeare's own sonnets (no. 116) which describes and praises the kind of love which admits and accepts change, whilst itself remaining steadfast.

'Let me not to the marriage of true minds
Admit impediments. Love is not love
Which alters when it alteration finds,
Or bends with the remover to remove.
O no, it is an ever-fixed mark

That looks on tempests and is never shaken;
It is the star to every wand'ring barque,
Whose worth's unknown although his height be taken.
Love's not time's fool, though rosy lips and cheeks
Within his bending sickle's compass come;
Love alters not with his brief hours and weeks,
But bears it out, even to the edge of doom.
If this be error and upon me proved,
I never writ, nor no man ever loved.'

13.a Look through your poetry books to find examples of love poetry which show the different ways we have of loving each other. You could copy out your favourites. Is there any one poet in particular that speaks to Othello's and Desdemona's plight?

LANGUAGE

14 *Shakespeare is famous for his language. He brought a very wide range of different kinds of words together, often drawing on ordinary people's ways of putting things, but also on the learned patterns originating in Latin and Greek. He was able to express himself in a way that no one had thought of before, and created phrases that will remain in our language for ever because of his use of comparisons with very down-to-earth or powerful pictures.*

These comparisons are called 'images' and a writer's use of them 'imagery'. There is an example in the very first scene, where Iago says, 'Even now, very now, an old black ram is tupping your white ewe!' The farmyard associations of the rampant ram and the passive ewe are meant to draw us worlds away from the loving reciprocity (both the man and the woman lovingly giving to each other) of Othello and Desdemona. If Iago can put a picture of animals in our mind, then it might make the lovers look like animals too.

14.a Find the image in Iago's speech as everyone disembarks on reaching Cyprus. Then explain how it clearly helps us to see what is in his mind, and what is in store for Cassio.

15 *Plays written at this time were mostly written in a patterned form of poetry called 'blank verse'. This was developed amongst actors and writers to enable them to move from the most ordinary lines of action to the highest moments of special feeling. Shakespeare undoubtedly developed this style of writing to its* *highest form. It had a regular rhythm of ten syllables to a line, stressed following unstressed. There were no rhymes, but the stress of the line was often used to give emphasis and bring out the special meaning.*

As you listen, it often sounds like the ordinary speech of prose - but when needed it can rise to unusually moving and powerful phrases. Here's an example from Act I Sc. III (printed in verse layout, not as in the script earlier in this book).

'Her father lov'd me; oft invited me;
Still question'd me the story of my life...
She lov'd me for the dangers I had pass'd;
And I lov'd her that she did pity them.'

Each line has ten beats and when you read it aloud you stress the even syllables. Try it.

Her FAther LOVed me, OFT inVITed ME.

This is called an ***Iambic Pentameter****. 'Iambic' is the technical term for a pair of syllables in which the first is weak and the second stressed (e.g. 'today') and 'pent-' means 'five' as in 'pentagon'. There are five weak-strong pairs in the line. In the script version printed in this book, the lines have not been printed in that way because it is a slimmed-down version. Here, though, is another short speech printed to show the blank verse as it would have been in Shakespeare's day. It is Othello's words from Act V Sc. II as he looks at Desdemona sleeping, and then at the candle by her bedside.*

'Put out the light, and then - put out the light!
If I quench thee, thou flaming minister,
I can again thy former light restore,
Should I repent me, but once put out thy light.'

15.a Try reading that speech aloud. Can you hear the weak-strong pattern? The last syllable of each line gains a slightly stronger stress. In this way Shakespeare influences the emphasis and expression of the actor.